CAMPING
JOURNAL

NAME: _____

PHONE: _____

Copyright © 2021 by **Premier Log Books Publishing**

All rights reserved. No part of this publication may be reproduced, distributed, or transmitted in any form or by any means, including photocopying, recording, or other electronic or mechanical methods, without the prior written permission of the publisher.

Campground: _____ Dates: _____

Location:_____

Travel to Campground: *Miles:*_____ *Time:*_____ *Cost:*_____

Weather/Temperature:_____

Campground Information

Name:_____

Address:_____

Phone:_____

Site#:_____ Site for next time:_____

Cost:_____ $ ☐ Day ☐ Week ☐ Month

GPS:_____

Rating: ★☆☆☆☆☆☆☆☆☆

Water pressure ★☆☆☆☆ Location ★☆☆☆☆

Cleanliness ★☆☆☆☆ Site size ★☆☆☆☆

Restrooms ★☆☆☆☆ Noise ★☆☆☆☆

Amenities:
- ☐ easy access
- ☐ water
- ☐ paved
- ☐ 15 amp
- ☐ shade
- ☐ store
- ☐ firewood
- ☐ security
- ☐ back-in
- ☐ pet friendly
- ☐ sewer
- ☐ 30 amp
- ☐ pool
- ☐ picnic table
- ☐ tv
- ☐ ice
- ☐ pull-through
- ☐ laundry
- ☐ electricity
- ☐ 50 amp
- ☐ restrooms
- ☐ fire ring
- ☐ wifi
- ☐ cafe

Activities:
- ☐ fishing
- ☐ lake
- ☐ fitness
- ☐ shuffleboard
- ☐ hiking
- ☐ river
- ☐ bike
- ☐ pickleball
- ☐ canoeing
- ☐ hot tub
- ☐ boat
- ☐ golf

Camped with:_____

_____

_____

People met:_____

_____

New friends:_____

_____

Places visited:_____

_____

_____

Visit/do next time:_____

_____

_____

Most memorable event:_____

_____

_____

Most fun things:_____

_____

_____

_____

Notes:_____

_____

_____

_____

_____

Drawing or favorite photo:

Campground:	Dates:

Location:_____

Travel to Campground: *Miles:*_____ *Time:*_____ *Cost:*_____

Weather/Temperature:_____

Campground Information

Name:_____

Address:_____

Phone:_____

Site#:_____ Site for next time:_____

Cost:_____ $ ☐ Day ☐ Week ☐ Month

GPS:_____

Rating: ★☆☆☆☆☆☆☆☆☆

Water pressure ★☆☆☆☆ Location ★☆☆☆☆

Cleanliness ★☆☆☆☆ Site size ★☆☆☆☆

Restrooms ★☆☆☆☆ Noise ★☆☆☆☆

Amenities:

☐ easy access ☐ back-in   ☐ pull-through
☐ water   ☐ pet friendly ☐ laundry
☐ paved   ☐ sewer   ☐ electricity
☐ 15 amp   ☐ 30 amp   ☐ 50 amp
☐ shade   ☐ pool   ☐ restrooms
☐ store   ☐ picnic table ☐ fire ring
☐ firewood   ☐ tv   ☐ wifi
☐ security   ☐ ice   ☐ cafe

Activities:

☐ fishing   ☐ hiking   ☐ canoeing
☐ lake   ☐ river   ☐ hot tub
☐ fitness   ☐ bike   ☐ boat
☐ shuffleboard ☐ pickleball   ☐ golf

Camped with:_____

_____

People met:_____

New friends:_____

Places visited:_____

_____

Visit/do next time:_____

_____

Most memorable event:_____

_____

_____

Most fun things:_____

_____

_____

Notes:_____

_____

_____

_____

_____

Drawing or favorite photo:

Campground: | Dates:

Location:_____

Travel to Campground: *Miles:*_____ *Time:*_____ *Cost:*_____

Weather/Temperature:_____

Campground Information

Name:_____

Address:_____

Phone:_____

Site#:_____ Site for next time:_____

Cost:_____ $ ☐ Day ☐ Week ☐ Month

GPS:_____

Rating: ★☆☆☆☆☆☆☆☆☆

Water pressure ★☆☆☆☆ Location ★☆☆☆☆

Cleanliness ★☆☆☆☆ Site size ★☆☆☆☆

Restrooms ★☆☆☆☆ Noise ★☆☆☆☆

Amenities:

☐ easy access ☐ back-in ☐ pull-through
☐ water ☐ pet friendly ☐ laundry
☐ paved ☐ sewer ☐ electricity
☐ 15 amp ☐ 30 amp ☐ 50 amp
☐ shade ☐ pool ☐ restrooms
☐ store ☐ picnic table ☐ fire ring
☐ firewood ☐ tv ☐ wifi
☐ security ☐ ice ☐ cafe

Activities:

☐ fishing ☐ hiking ☐ canoeing
☐ lake ☐ river ☐ hot tub
☐ fitness ☐ bike ☐ boat
☐ shuffleboard ☐ pickleball ☐ golf

Camped with:_____

_____

People met:_____

New friends:_____

Places visited:_____

_____

Visit/do next time:_____

_____

Most memorable event:_____

_____

_____

Most fun things:_____

_____

_____

_____

Notes:_____

_____

_____

_____

_____

_____

Drawing or favorite photo:

Campground:	Dates:

Location:_____

Travel to Campground: *Miles:*_____ *Time:*_____ *Cost:*_____

Weather/Temperature:_____

Campground Information

Name:_____

Address:_____

Phone:_____

Site#:_____ Site for next time:_____

Cost:_____ $ ☐ Day ☐ Week ☐ Month

GPS:_____

Rating: ★☆☆☆☆☆☆☆☆☆

Water pressure ★☆☆☆☆ Location ★☆☆☆☆

Cleanliness ★☆☆☆☆ Site size ★☆☆☆☆

Restrooms ★☆☆☆☆ Noise ★☆☆☆☆

Amenities:

☐ easy access ☐ back-in ☐ pull-through
☐ water ☐ pet friendly ☐ laundry
☐ paved ☐ sewer ☐ electricity
☐ 15 amp ☐ 30 amp ☐ 50 amp
☐ shade ☐ pool ☐ restrooms
☐ store ☐ picnic table ☐ fire ring
☐ firewood ☐ tv ☐ wifi
☐ security ☐ ice ☐ cafe

Activities:

☐ fishing ☐ hiking ☐ canoeing
☐ lake ☐ river ☐ hot tub
☐ fitness ☐ bike ☐ boat
☐ shuffleboard ☐ pickleball ☐ golf

Camped with:_____

_____

People met:_____

New friends:_____

Places visited:_____

_____

Visit/do next time:_____

_____

Most memorable event:_____

_____

Most fun things:_____

_____

_____

Notes:_____

_____

_____

_____

Drawing or favorite photo:

Campground: _____ Dates: _____

Location:_____

Travel to Campground: *Miles:*_____ *Time:*_____ *Cost:*_____

Weather/Temperature:_____

Campground Information

Name:_____

Address:_____

Phone:_____

Site#:_____ Site for next time:_____

Cost:_____ $ ☐ Day ☐ Week ☐ Month

GPS:_____

Rating: ★☆☆☆☆☆☆☆☆☆

Water pressure ★☆☆☆☆ Location ★☆☆☆☆

Cleanliness ★☆☆☆☆ Site size ★☆☆☆☆

Restrooms ★☆☆☆☆ Noise ★☆☆☆☆

Amenities:

☐ easy access ☐ back-in ☐ pull-through
☐ water ☐ pet friendly ☐ laundry
☐ paved ☐ sewer ☐ electricity
☐ 15 amp ☐ 30 amp ☐ 50 amp
☐ shade ☐ pool ☐ restrooms
☐ store ☐ picnic table ☐ fire ring
☐ firewood ☐ tv ☐ wifi
☐ security ☐ ice ☐ cafe

Activities:

☐ fishing ☐ hiking ☐ canoeing
☐ lake ☐ river ☐ hot tub
☐ fitness ☐ bike ☐ boat
☐ shuffleboard ☐ pickleball ☐ golf

Camped with:_____

_____

People met:_____

_____

New friends:_____

Places visited:_____

_____

Visit/do next time:_____

_____

Most memorable event:_____

_____

_____

Most fun things:_____

_____

_____

_____

Notes:_____

_____

_____

_____

_____

Drawing or favorite photo:

Campground: _____ Dates: _____

Location:_____

Travel to Campground: *Miles:*_____ *Time:*_____ *Cost:*_____

Weather/Temperature:_____

Campground Information

Name:_____

Address:_____
_____

Phone:_____

Site#:_____ Site for next time:_____

Cost:_____ $ ☐ Day ☐ Week ☐ Month

GPS:_____

Rating: ★☆☆☆☆☆☆☆☆☆

Water pressure ★☆☆☆☆ Location ★☆☆☆☆

Cleanliness ★☆☆☆☆ Site size ★☆☆☆☆

Restrooms ★☆☆☆☆ Noise ★☆☆☆☆

Amenities:

☐ easy access ☐ back-in ☐ pull-through
☐ water ☐ pet friendly ☐ laundry
☐ paved ☐ sewer ☐ electricity
☐ 15 amp ☐ 30 amp ☐ 50 amp
☐ shade ☐ pool ☐ restrooms
☐ store ☐ picnic table ☐ fire ring
☐ firewood ☐ tv ☐ wifi
☐ security ☐ ice ☐ cafe

Activities:

☐ fishing ☐ hiking ☐ canoeing
☐ lake ☐ river ☐ hot tub
☐ fitness ☐ bike ☐ boat
☐ shuffleboard ☐ pickleball ☐ golf

Camped with:_____
_____
_____

People met:_____
_____

New friends:_____
_____

Places visited:_____
_____
_____

Visit/do next time:_____
_____
_____

Most memorable event:_____

_____

_____

Most fun things:_____

_____

_____

_____

Notes:_____

_____

_____

_____

_____

Drawing or favorite photo:

Campground: _____ Dates: _____

Location: _____

Travel to Campground: *Miles:* _____ *Time:* _____ *Cost:* _____

Weather/Temperature: _____

Campground Information

Name: _____

Address: _____

Phone: _____

Site#: _____ Site for next time: _____

Cost: _____ $ ☐ Day ☐ Week ☐ Month

GPS: _____

Rating: ★☆☆☆☆☆☆☆☆☆

Water pressure ★☆☆☆☆ Location ★☆☆☆☆

Cleanliness ★☆☆☆☆ Site size ★☆☆☆☆

Restrooms ★☆☆☆☆ Noise ★☆☆☆☆

Amenities:

☐ easy access ☐ back-in ☐ pull-through
☐ water ☐ pet friendly ☐ laundry
☐ paved ☐ sewer ☐ electricity
☐ 15 amp ☐ 30 amp ☐ 50 amp
☐ shade ☐ pool ☐ restrooms
☐ store ☐ picnic table ☐ fire ring
☐ firewood ☐ tv ☐ wifi
☐ security ☐ ice ☐ cafe

Activities:

☐ fishing ☐ hiking ☐ canoeing
☐ lake ☐ river ☐ hot tub
☐ fitness ☐ bike ☐ boat
☐ shuffleboard ☐ pickleball ☐ golf

Camped with: _____

_____

People met: _____

New friends: _____

Places visited: _____

_____

Visit/do next time: _____

_____

Most memorable event:_____

_____

Most fun things:_____

_____

_____

Notes:_____

_____

_____

_____

Drawing or favorite photo:

Campground:	Dates:

Location:_____

Travel to Campground: *Miles:*_____ *Time:*_____ *Cost:*_____

Weather/Temperature:_____

Campground Information

Name:_____

Address:_____

Phone:_____

Site#:_____ Site for next time:_____

Cost:_____ $ ☐ Day ☐ Week ☐ Month

GPS:_____

Rating: ★☆☆☆☆☆☆☆☆☆

Water pressure ★☆☆☆☆ Location ★☆☆☆☆

Cleanliness ★☆☆☆☆ Site size ★☆☆☆☆

Restrooms ★☆☆☆☆ Noise ★☆☆☆☆

Amenities:

☐ easy access	☐ back-in	☐ pull-through
☐ water	☐ pet friendly	☐ laundry
☐ paved	☐ sewer	☐ electricity
☐ 15 amp	☐ 30 amp	☐ 50 amp
☐ shade	☐ pool	☐ restrooms
☐ store	☐ picnic table	☐ fire ring
☐ firewood	☐ tv	☐ wifi
☐ security	☐ ice	☐ cafe

Activities:

☐ fishing	☐ hiking	☐ canoeing
☐ lake	☐ river	☐ hot tub
☐ fitness	☐ bike	☐ boat
☐ shuffleboard	☐ pickleball	☐ golf

Camped with:_____

_____

_____

People met:_____

_____

New friends:_____

_____

Places visited:_____

_____

_____

Visit/do next time:_____

_____

_____

Most memorable event:_____

_____

_____

Most fun things:_____

_____

_____

_____

Notes:_____

_____

_____

_____

_____

_____

Drawing or favorite photo:

Campground: Dates:

Location:_____

Travel to Campground: *Miles:*_____ *Time:*_____ *Cost:*_____

Weather/Temperature:_____

Campground Information

Name:_____

Address:_____

Phone:_____

Site#:_____ Site for next time:_____

Cost:_____ $ ☐ Day ☐ Week ☐ Month

GPS:_____

Rating: ★☆☆☆☆☆☆☆☆☆

Water pressure ★☆☆☆☆ Location ★☆☆☆☆

Cleanliness ★☆☆☆☆ Site size ★☆☆☆☆

Restrooms ★☆☆☆☆ Noise ★☆☆☆☆

Amenities:

☐ easy access ☐ back-in ☐ pull-through
☐ water ☐ pet friendly ☐ laundry
☐ paved ☐ sewer ☐ electricity
☐ 15 amp ☐ 30 amp ☐ 50 amp
☐ shade ☐ pool ☐ restrooms
☐ store ☐ picnic table ☐ fire ring
☐ firewood ☐ tv ☐ wifi
☐ security ☐ ice ☐ cafe

Activities:

☐ fishing ☐ hiking ☐ canoeing
☐ lake ☐ river ☐ hot tub
☐ fitness ☐ bike ☐ boat
☐ shuffleboard ☐ pickleball ☐ golf

Camped with:_____

_____

_____

People met:_____

_____

New friends:_____

_____

Places visited:_____

_____

_____

Visit/do next time:_____

_____

_____

Most memorable event:_____

_____

_____

Most fun things:_____

_____

_____

_____

Notes:_____

_____

_____

_____

_____

Drawing or favorite photo:

Campground: Dates:

Location:_____

Travel to Campground: *Miles:*_____ *Time:*_____ *Cost:*_____

Weather/Temperature:_____

Campground Information

Name:_____

Address:_____

Phone:_____

Site#:_____ Site for next time:_____

Cost:_____ $ ☐ Day ☐ Week ☐ Month

GPS:_____

Rating: ★☆☆☆☆☆☆☆☆☆

Water pressure ★☆☆☆☆   Location ★☆☆☆☆

Cleanliness   ★☆☆☆☆   Site size ★☆☆☆☆

Restrooms   ★☆☆☆☆   Noise   ★☆☆☆☆

Amenities:

☐ easy access	☐ back-in	☐ pull-through
☐ water	☐ pet friendly	☐ laundry
☐ paved	☐ sewer	☐ electricity
☐ 15 amp	☐ 30 amp	☐ 50 amp
☐ shade	☐ pool	☐ restrooms
☐ store	☐ picnic table	☐ fire ring
☐ firewood	☐ tv	☐ wifi
☐ security	☐ ice	☐ cafe

Activities:

☐ fishing	☐ hiking	☐ canoeing
☐ lake	☐ river	☐ hot tub
☐ fitness	☐ bike	☐ boat
☐ shuffleboard	☐ pickleball	☐ golf

Camped with:_____

_____

_____

People met:_____

_____

New friends:_____

_____

Places visited:_____

_____

_____

Visit/do next time:_____

_____

_____

Most memorable event:_____

_____

_____

Most fun things:_____

_____

_____

_____

Notes:_____

_____

_____

_____

_____

Drawing or favorite photo:

Campground: Dates:

Location:_____

Travel to Campground: *Miles:*_____ *Time:*_____ *Cost:*_____

Weather/Temperature:_____

Campground Information

Name:_____

Address:_____

Phone:_____

Site#:_____ Site for next time:_____

Cost:_____ $ ☐ Day ☐ Week ☐ Month

GPS:_____

Rating: ★☆☆☆☆☆☆☆☆☆

Water pressure ★☆☆☆☆ Location ★☆☆☆☆

Cleanliness   ★☆☆☆☆ Site size ★☆☆☆☆

Restrooms   ★☆☆☆☆ Noise   ★☆☆☆☆

Amenities:

☐ easy access   ☐ back-in   ☐ pull-through
☐ water   ☐ pet friendly ☐ laundry
☐ paved   ☐ sewer   ☐ electricity
☐ 15 amp   ☐ 30 amp   ☐ 50 amp
☐ shade   ☐ pool   ☐ restrooms
☐ store   ☐ picnic table ☐ fire ring
☐ firewood   ☐ tv   ☐ wifi
☐ security   ☐ ice   ☐ cafe

Activities:

☐ fishing   ☐ hiking   ☐ canoeing
☐ lake   ☐ river   ☐ hot tub
☐ fitness   ☐ bike   ☐ boat
☐ shuffleboard ☐ pickleball   ☐ golf

Camped with:_____

_____

People met:_____

New friends:_____

Places visited:_____

_____

Visit/do next time:_____

_____

_____

Most memorable event:_____

_____

_____

Most fun things:_____

_____

_____

_____

Notes:_____

_____

_____

_____

_____

Drawing or favorite photo:

Campground: _____ Dates: _____

Location:_____

Travel to Campground: *Miles:*_____ *Time:*_____ *Cost:*_____

Weather/Temperature:_____

Campground Information

Name:_____

Address:_____

Phone:_____

Site#:_____ Site for next time:_____

Cost:_____ $ ☐ Day ☐ Week ☐ Month

GPS:_____

Rating: ★☆☆☆☆☆☆☆☆☆

Water pressure ★☆☆☆☆ Location ★☆☆☆☆

Cleanliness ★☆☆☆☆ Site size ★☆☆☆☆

Restrooms ★☆☆☆☆ Noise ★☆☆☆☆

Amenities:

☐ easy access ☐ back-in ☐ pull-through
☐ water ☐ pet friendly ☐ laundry
☐ paved ☐ sewer ☐ electricity
☐ 15 amp ☐ 30 amp ☐ 50 amp
☐ shade ☐ pool ☐ restrooms
☐ store ☐ picnic table ☐ fire ring
☐ firewood ☐ tv ☐ wifi
☐ security ☐ ice ☐ cafe

Activities:

☐ fishing ☐ hiking ☐ canoeing
☐ lake ☐ river ☐ hot tub
☐ fitness ☐ bike ☐ boat
☐ shuffleboard ☐ pickleball ☐ golf

Camped with:_____

_____

_____

People met:_____

_____

New friends:_____

_____

Places visited:_____

_____

_____

Visit/do next time:_____

_____

_____

Most memorable event:_____

_____

Most fun things:_____

_____

_____

Notes:_____

_____

_____

_____

_____

Drawing or favorite photo:

Campground: Dates:

Location:_____

Travel to Campground: *Miles:*_____ *Time:*_____ *Cost:*_____

Weather/Temperature:_____

Campground Information

Name:_____

Address:_____

Phone:_____

Site#:_____ Site for next time:_____

Cost:_____ $ ☐ Day ☐ Week ☐ Month

GPS:_____

Rating: ★☆☆☆☆☆☆☆☆☆

Water pressure ★☆☆☆☆ Location ★☆☆☆☆

Cleanliness ★☆☆☆☆ Site size ★☆☆☆☆

Restrooms ★☆☆☆☆ Noise ★☆☆☆☆

Amenities:

☐ easy access ☐ back-in ☐ pull-through
☐ water ☐ pet friendly ☐ laundry
☐ paved ☐ sewer ☐ electricity
☐ 15 amp ☐ 30 amp ☐ 50 amp
☐ shade ☐ pool ☐ restrooms
☐ store ☐ picnic table ☐ fire ring
☐ firewood ☐ tv ☐ wifi
☐ security ☐ ice ☐ cafe

Activities:

☐ fishing ☐ hiking ☐ canoeing
☐ lake ☐ river ☐ hot tub
☐ fitness ☐ bike ☐ boat
☐ shuffleboard ☐ pickleball ☐ golf

Camped with:_____
_____
_____

People met:_____
_____

New friends:_____
_____

Places visited:_____
_____
_____

Visit/do next time:_____
_____
_____

Most memorable event: _____

_____

_____

Most fun things: _____

_____

_____

_____

Notes: _____

_____

_____

_____

_____

Drawing or favorite photo:

Campground: _____ Dates: _____

Location: _____

Travel to Campground: *Miles:* _____ *Time:* _____ *Cost:* _____

Weather/Temperature: _____

Campground Information

Name: _____

Address: _____

Phone: _____

Site#: _____ Site for next time: _____

Cost: _____ $ ☐ Day ☐ Week ☐ Month

GPS: _____

Rating: ★☆☆☆☆☆☆☆☆☆

Water pressure ★☆☆☆☆ Location ★☆☆☆☆

Cleanliness ★☆☆☆☆ Site size ★☆☆☆☆

Restrooms ★☆☆☆☆ Noise ★☆☆☆☆

Amenities:

☐ easy access ☐ back-in ☐ pull-through
☐ water ☐ pet friendly ☐ laundry
☐ paved ☐ sewer ☐ electricity
☐ 15 amp ☐ 30 amp ☐ 50 amp
☐ shade ☐ pool ☐ restrooms
☐ store ☐ picnic table ☐ fire ring
☐ firewood ☐ tv ☐ wifi
☐ security ☐ ice ☐ cafe

Activities:

☐ fishing ☐ hiking ☐ canoeing
☐ lake ☐ river ☐ hot tub
☐ fitness ☐ bike ☐ boat
☐ shuffleboard ☐ pickleball ☐ golf

Camped with: _____

_____

People met: _____

New friends: _____

Places visited: _____

Visit/do next time: _____

_____

Most memorable event:_____
_____

Most fun things:_____
_____
_____

Notes:_____
_____
_____
_____

Drawing or favorite photo:

Campground:	Dates:

Location:_____

Travel to Campground: *Miles:*_____ *Time:*_____ *Cost:*_____

Weather/Temperature:_____

Campground Information

Name:_____

Address:_____

Phone:_____

Site#:_____ Site for next time:_____

Cost:_____ $ ☐ Day ☐ Week ☐ Month

GPS:_____

Rating: ★☆☆☆☆☆☆☆☆☆

Water pressure ★☆☆☆☆ Location ★☆☆☆☆

Cleanliness ★☆☆☆☆ Site size ★☆☆☆☆

Restrooms ★☆☆☆☆ Noise ★☆☆☆☆

Amenities:

☐ easy access ☐ back-in ☐ pull-through
☐ water ☐ pet friendly ☐ laundry
☐ paved ☐ sewer ☐ electricity
☐ 15 amp ☐ 30 amp ☐ 50 amp
☐ shade ☐ pool ☐ restrooms
☐ store ☐ picnic table ☐ fire ring
☐ firewood ☐ tv ☐ wifi
☐ security ☐ ice ☐ cafe

Activities:

☐ fishing ☐ hiking ☐ canoeing
☐ lake ☐ river ☐ hot tub
☐ fitness ☐ bike ☐ boat
☐ shuffleboard ☐ pickleball ☐ golf

Camped with:_____

_____

People met:_____

New friends:_____

Places visited:_____

_____

Visit/do next time:_____

_____

Most memorable event:_____

_____

_____

Most fun things:_____

_____

_____

_____

Notes:_____

_____

_____

_____

_____

Drawing or favorite photo:

Campground: Dates:

Location:_____

Travel to Campground: *Miles:*_____ *Time:*_____ *Cost:*_____

Weather/Temperature:_____

Campground Information

Name:_____	**Amenities:**
Address:_____	☐ easy access ☐ back-in ☐ pull-through
Phone:_____	☐ water ☐ pet friendly ☐ laundry
Site#:_____ Site for next time:_____	☐ paved ☐ sewer ☐ electricity
Cost:_____ $ ☐ Day ☐ Week ☐ Month	☐ 15 amp ☐ 30 amp ☐ 50 amp
GPS:_____	☐ shade ☐ pool ☐ restrooms

Amenities:

☐ easy access ☐ back-in ☐ pull-through
☐ water ☐ pet friendly ☐ laundry
☐ paved ☐ sewer ☐ electricity
☐ 15 amp ☐ 30 amp ☐ 50 amp
☐ shade ☐ pool ☐ restrooms
☐ store ☐ picnic table ☐ fire ring
☐ firewood ☐ tv ☐ wifi
☐ security ☐ ice ☐ cafe

Rating: ★☆☆☆☆☆☆☆☆☆

Water pressure ★☆☆☆☆ Location ★☆☆☆☆
Cleanliness ★☆☆☆☆ Site size ★☆☆☆☆
Restrooms ★☆☆☆☆ Noise ★☆☆☆☆

Activities:

☐ fishing ☐ hiking ☐ canoeing
☐ lake ☐ river ☐ hot tub
☐ fitness ☐ bike ☐ boat
☐ shuffleboard ☐ pickleball ☐ golf

Camped with:_____
_____
_____

People met:_____
_____

New friends:_____
_____

Places visited:_____
_____
_____

Visit/do next time:_____
_____
_____

Most memorable event:_____

_____

Most fun things:_____

_____

_____

Notes:_____

_____

_____

_____

_____

Drawing or favorite photo:

Campground:		Dates:

Location:_____

Travel to Campground: *Miles:*_____ *Time:*_____ *Cost:*_____

Weather/Temperature:_____

Campground Information

Name:_____

Address:_____

Phone:_____

Site#:_____ Site for next time:_____

Cost:_____ $ ☐ Day ☐ Week ☐ Month

GPS:_____

Rating: ★☆☆☆☆☆☆☆☆☆

Water pressure ★☆☆☆☆ Location ★☆☆☆☆

Cleanliness ★☆☆☆☆ Site size ★☆☆☆☆

Restrooms ★☆☆☆☆ Noise ★☆☆☆☆

Amenities:

☐ easy access ☐ back-in ☐ pull-through
☐ water ☐ pet friendly ☐ laundry
☐ paved ☐ sewer ☐ electricity
☐ 15 amp ☐ 30 amp ☐ 50 amp
☐ shade ☐ pool ☐ restrooms
☐ store ☐ picnic table ☐ fire ring
☐ firewood ☐ tv ☐ wifi
☐ security ☐ ice ☐ cafe

Activities:

☐ fishing ☐ hiking ☐ canoeing
☐ lake ☐ river ☐ hot tub
☐ fitness ☐ bike ☐ boat
☐ shuffleboard ☐ pickleball ☐ golf

Camped with:_____

_____

_____

People met:_____

_____

New friends:_____

_____

Places visited:_____

_____

_____

Visit/do next time:_____

_____

_____

Most memorable event:_____

_____

_____

Most fun things:_____

_____

_____

_____

Notes:_____

_____

_____

_____

_____

Drawing or favorite photo:

Campground: Dates:

Location:_____

Travel to Campground: *Miles:*_____ *Time:*_____ *Cost:*_____

Weather/Temperature:_____

Campground Information

Name:_____

Address:_____

Phone:_____

Site#:_____ Site for next time:_____

Cost:_____ $ ☐ Day ☐ Week ☐ Month

GPS:_____

Rating: ★☆☆☆☆☆☆☆☆☆

Water pressure ★☆☆☆☆   Location   ★☆☆☆☆

Cleanliness   ★☆☆☆☆   Site size   ★☆☆☆☆

Restrooms   ★☆☆☆☆   Noise   ★☆☆☆☆

Amenities:

☐ easy access   ☐ back-in   ☐ pull-through
☐ water   ☐ pet friendly   ☐ laundry
☐ paved   ☐ sewer   ☐ electricity
☐ 15 amp   ☐ 30 amp   ☐ 50 amp
☐ shade   ☐ pool   ☐ restrooms
☐ store   ☐ picnic table   ☐ fire ring
☐ firewood   ☐ tv   ☐ wifi
☐ security   ☐ ice   ☐ cafe

Activities:

☐ fishing   ☐ hiking   ☐ canoeing
☐ lake   ☐ river   ☐ hot tub
☐ fitness   ☐ bike   ☐ boat
☐ shuffleboard   ☐ pickleball   ☐ golf

Camped with:_____

_____

People met:_____

New friends:_____

Places visited:_____

_____

Visit/do next time:_____

_____

Most memorable event:_____

_____

_____

Most fun things:_____

_____

_____

_____

Notes:_____

_____

_____

_____

_____

_____

Drawing or favorite photo:

Campground: _____ Dates: _____

Location:_____

Travel to Campground: *Miles:*_____ *Time:*_____ *Cost:*_____

Weather/Temperature:_____

Campground Information

Name:_____

Address:_____

Phone:_____

Site#:_____ Site for next time:_____

Cost:_____ $ ☐ Day ☐ Week ☐ Month

GPS:_____

Rating: ★☆☆☆☆☆☆☆☆☆

Water pressure ★☆☆☆☆ Location ★☆☆☆☆

Cleanliness ★☆☆☆☆ Site size ★☆☆☆☆

Restrooms ★☆☆☆☆ Noise ★☆☆☆☆

Amenities:

☐ easy access ☐ back-in ☐ pull-through
☐ water ☐ pet friendly ☐ laundry
☐ paved ☐ sewer ☐ electricity
☐ 15 amp ☐ 30 amp ☐ 50 amp
☐ shade ☐ pool ☐ restrooms
☐ store ☐ picnic table ☐ fire ring
☐ firewood ☐ tv ☐ wifi
☐ security ☐ ice ☐ cafe

Activities:

☐ fishing ☐ hiking ☐ canoeing
☐ lake ☐ river ☐ hot tub
☐ fitness ☐ bike ☐ boat
☐ shuffleboard ☐ pickleball ☐ golf

Camped with:_____

_____

_____

People met:_____

_____

New friends:_____

_____

Places visited:_____

_____

_____

Visit/do next time:_____

_____

_____

Most memorable event:_____

_____

Most fun things:_____

_____

_____

Notes:_____

_____

_____

_____

_____

Drawing or favorite photo:

Campground:	Dates:

Location:_____

Travel to Campground: *Miles:*_____ *Time:*_____ *Cost:*_____

Weather/Temperature:_____

Campground Information

Name:_____

Address:_____

Phone:_____

Site#:_____ Site for next time:_____

Cost:_____ $ ☐ Day ☐ Week ☐ Month

GPS:_____

Rating: ★☆☆☆☆☆☆☆☆☆

Water pressure ★☆☆☆☆ Location ★☆☆☆☆

Cleanliness ★☆☆☆☆ Site size ★☆☆☆☆

Restrooms ★☆☆☆☆ Noise ★☆☆☆☆

Amenities:

☐ easy access ☐ back-in ☐ pull-through
☐ water ☐ pet friendly ☐ laundry
☐ paved ☐ sewer ☐ electricity
☐ 15 amp ☐ 30 amp ☐ 50 amp
☐ shade ☐ pool ☐ restrooms
☐ store ☐ picnic table ☐ fire ring
☐ firewood ☐ tv ☐ wifi
☐ security ☐ ice ☐ cafe

Activities:

☐ fishing ☐ hiking ☐ canoeing
☐ lake ☐ river ☐ hot tub
☐ fitness ☐ bike ☐ boat
☐ shuffleboard ☐ pickleball ☐ golf

Camped with:_____

_____

_____

People met:_____

_____

New friends:_____

_____

Places visited:_____

_____

_____

Visit/do next time:_____

_____

_____

Most memorable event:_____

_____

Most fun things:_____

_____

_____

Notes:_____

_____

_____

_____

_____

Drawing or favorite photo:

Campground: Dates:

Location:_____

Travel to Campground: *Miles:*_____ *Time:*_____ *Cost:*_____

Weather/Temperature:_____

Campground Information

Name:_____

Address:_____

Phone:_____

Site#:_____ Site for next time:_____

Cost:_____ $ ☐ Day ☐ Week ☐ Month

GPS:_____

Rating: ★☆☆☆☆☆☆☆☆☆

Water pressure ★☆☆☆☆ Location ★☆☆☆☆

Cleanliness ★☆☆☆☆ Site size ★☆☆☆☆

Restrooms ★☆☆☆☆ Noise ★☆☆☆☆

Amenities:

☐ easy access   ☐ back-in   ☐ pull-through
☐ water   ☐ pet friendly   ☐ laundry
☐ paved   ☐ sewer   ☐ electricity
☐ 15 amp   ☐ 30 amp   ☐ 50 amp
☐ shade   ☐ pool   ☐ restrooms
☐ store   ☐ picnic table   ☐ fire ring
☐ firewood   ☐ tv   ☐ wifi
☐ security   ☐ ice   ☐ cafe

Activities:

☐ fishing   ☐ hiking   ☐ canoeing
☐ lake   ☐ river   ☐ hot tub
☐ fitness   ☐ bike   ☐ boat
☐ shuffleboard ☐ pickleball   ☐ golf

Camped with:_____

_____

_____

People met:_____

_____

New friends:_____

_____

Places visited:_____

_____

_____

Visit/do next time:_____

_____

_____

Most memorable event:_____

_____

Most fun things:_____

_____

_____

_____

Notes:_____

_____

_____

_____

_____

Drawing or favorite photo:

Campground:

Dates:

Location:_____

Travel to Campground: *Miles:*_____ *Time:*_____ *Cost:*_____

Weather/Temperature:_____

Campground Information

Name:_____

Address:_____

Phone:_____

Site#:_____ Site for next time:_____

Cost:_____ $ ☐ Day ☐ Week ☐ Month

GPS:_____

Rating: ★☆☆☆☆☆☆☆☆☆

Water pressure ★☆☆☆☆ Location ★☆☆☆☆

Cleanliness ★☆☆☆☆ Site size ★☆☆☆☆

Restrooms ★☆☆☆☆ Noise ★☆☆☆☆

Amenities:

☐ easy access ☐ back-in ☐ pull-through
☐ water ☐ pet friendly ☐ laundry
☐ paved ☐ sewer ☐ electricity
☐ 15 amp ☐ 30 amp ☐ 50 amp
☐ shade ☐ pool ☐ restrooms
☐ store ☐ picnic table ☐ fire ring
☐ firewood ☐ tv ☐ wifi
☐ security ☐ ice ☐ cafe

Activities:

☐ fishing ☐ hiking ☐ canoeing
☐ lake ☐ river ☐ hot tub
☐ fitness ☐ bike ☐ boat
☐ shuffleboard ☐ pickleball ☐ golf

Camped with:_____

_____

_____

People met:_____

_____

New friends:_____

_____

Places visited:_____

_____

_____

Visit/do next time:_____

_____

_____

Most memorable event:_____

_____

_____

Most fun things:_____

_____

_____

Notes:_____

_____

_____

_____

_____

Drawing or favorite photo:

Campground: Dates:

Location:_____

Travel to Campground: *Miles:*_____ *Time:*_____ *Cost:*_____

Weather/Temperature:_____

Campground Information

Name:_____

Address:_____

Phone:_____

Site#:_____ Site for next time:_____

Cost:_____ $ ☐ Day ☐ Week ☐ Month

GPS:_____

Rating: ★☆☆☆☆☆☆☆☆☆

Water pressure ★☆☆☆☆ Location ★☆☆☆☆

Cleanliness ★☆☆☆☆ Site size ★☆☆☆☆

Restrooms ★☆☆☆☆ Noise ★☆☆☆☆

Amenities:

☐ easy access ☐ back-in ☐ pull-through
☐ water ☐ pet friendly ☐ laundry
☐ paved ☐ sewer ☐ electricity
☐ 15 amp ☐ 30 amp ☐ 50 amp
☐ shade ☐ pool ☐ restrooms
☐ store ☐ picnic table ☐ fire ring
☐ firewood ☐ tv ☐ wifi
☐ security ☐ ice ☐ cafe

Activities:

☐ fishing ☐ hiking ☐ canoeing
☐ lake ☐ river ☐ hot tub
☐ fitness ☐ bike ☐ boat
☐ shuffleboard ☐ pickleball ☐ golf

Camped with:_____

_____

_____

People met:_____

_____

New friends:_____

_____

Places visited:_____

_____

_____

Visit/do next time:_____

_____

_____

Most memorable event:_____

_____

Most fun things:_____

_____

_____

Notes:_____

_____

_____

_____

Drawing or favorite photo:

Campground:	Dates:

Location:_____

Travel to Campground: *Miles:*_____ *Time:*_____ *Cost:*_____

Weather/Temperature:_____

Campground Information

Name:_____

Address:_____

Phone:_____

Site#:_____ Site for next time:_____

Cost:_____ $ ☐ Day ☐ Week ☐ Month

GPS:_____

Rating: ★☆☆☆☆☆☆☆☆☆

Water pressure ★☆☆☆☆ Location ★☆☆☆☆

Cleanliness ★☆☆☆☆ Site size ★☆☆☆☆

Restrooms ★☆☆☆☆ Noise ★☆☆☆☆

Amenities:

☐ easy access ☐ back-in ☐ pull-through
☐ water ☐ pet friendly ☐ laundry
☐ paved ☐ sewer ☐ electricity
☐ 15 amp ☐ 30 amp ☐ 50 amp
☐ shade ☐ pool ☐ restrooms
☐ store ☐ picnic table ☐ fire ring
☐ firewood ☐ tv ☐ wifi
☐ security ☐ ice ☐ cafe

Activities:

☐ fishing ☐ hiking ☐ canoeing
☐ lake ☐ river ☐ hot tub
☐ fitness ☐ bike ☐ boat
☐ shuffleboard ☐ pickleball ☐ golf

Camped with:_____

_____

_____

People met:_____

_____

New friends:_____

_____

Places visited:_____

_____

_____

Visit/do next time:_____

_____

_____

Most memorable event:_____

_____

_____

Most fun things:_____

_____

_____

_____

Notes:_____

_____

_____

_____

_____

_____

Drawing or favorite photo:

Campground: Dates:

Location:_____

Travel to Campground: *Miles:*_____ *Time:*_____ *Cost:*_____

Weather/Temperature:_____

Campground Information

Name:_____

Address:_____

Phone:_____

Site#:_____ Site for next time:_____

Cost:_____ $ ☐ Day ☐ Week ☐ Month

GPS:_____

Rating: ★☆☆☆☆☆☆☆☆☆

Water pressure ★☆☆☆☆ Location ★☆☆☆☆

Cleanliness ★☆☆☆☆ Site size ★☆☆☆☆

Restrooms ★☆☆☆☆ Noise ★☆☆☆☆

Amenities:

☐ easy access	☐ back-in	☐ pull-through
☐ water	☐ pet friendly	☐ laundry
☐ paved	☐ sewer	☐ electricity
☐ 15 amp	☐ 30 amp	☐ 50 amp
☐ shade	☐ pool	☐ restrooms
☐ store	☐ picnic table	☐ fire ring
☐ firewood	☐ tv	☐ wifi
☐ security	☐ ice	☐ cafe

Activities:

☐ fishing	☐ hiking	☐ canoeing
☐ lake	☐ river	☐ hot tub
☐ fitness	☐ bike	☐ boat
☐ shuffleboard	☐ pickleball	☐ golf

Camped with:_____

_____

_____

People met:_____

_____

New friends:_____

Places visited:_____

_____

_____

Visit/do next time:_____

_____

_____

Most memorable event:_____

_____

_____

Most fun things:_____

_____

_____

_____

Notes:_____

_____

_____

_____

_____

Drawing or favorite photo:

Campground:	Dates:

Location:_____

Travel to Campground: *Miles:*_____ *Time:*_____ *Cost:*_____

Weather/Temperature:_____

Campground Information

Name:_____

Address:_____

Phone:_____

Site#:_____ Site for next time:_____

Cost:_____ $ ☐ Day ☐ Week ☐ Month

GPS:_____

Rating: ★☆☆☆☆☆☆☆☆☆

Water pressure ★☆☆☆☆ Location ★☆☆☆☆

Cleanliness ★☆☆☆☆ Site size ★☆☆☆☆

Restrooms ★☆☆☆☆ Noise ★☆☆☆☆

Amenities:

☐ easy access ☐ back-in ☐ pull-through
☐ water ☐ pet friendly ☐ laundry
☐ paved ☐ sewer ☐ electricity
☐ 15 amp ☐ 30 amp ☐ 50 amp
☐ shade ☐ pool ☐ restrooms
☐ store ☐ picnic table ☐ fire ring
☐ firewood ☐ tv ☐ wifi
☐ security ☐ ice ☐ cafe

Activities:

☐ fishing ☐ hiking ☐ canoeing
☐ lake ☐ river ☐ hot tub
☐ fitness ☐ bike ☐ boat
☐ shuffleboard ☐ pickleball ☐ golf

Camped with:_____

_____

People met:_____

New friends:_____

Places visited:_____

_____

Visit/do next time:_____

_____

Most memorable event:_____

_____

Most fun things:_____

_____

_____

Notes:_____

_____

_____

_____

_____

Drawing or favorite photo:

Campground: Dates:

Location:_____

Travel to Campground: *Miles:*_____ *Time:*_____ *Cost:*_____

Weather/Temperature:_____

Campground Information

Name:_____

Address:_____

Phone:_____

Site#:_____ Site for next time:_____

Cost:_____ $ ☐ Day ☐ Week ☐ Month

GPS:_____

Rating: ★☆☆☆☆☆☆☆☆☆

Water pressure ★☆☆☆☆   Location ★☆☆☆☆

Cleanliness ★☆☆☆☆   Site size ★☆☆☆☆

Restrooms ★☆☆☆☆   Noise ★☆☆☆☆

Amenities:

☐ easy access   ☐ back-in   ☐ pull-through
☐ water   ☐ pet friendly   ☐ laundry
☐ paved   ☐ sewer   ☐ electricity
☐ 15 amp   ☐ 30 amp   ☐ 50 amp
☐ shade   ☐ pool   ☐ restrooms
☐ store   ☐ picnic table   ☐ fire ring
☐ firewood   ☐ tv   ☐ wifi
☐ security   ☐ ice   ☐ cafe

Activities:

☐ fishing   ☐ hiking   ☐ canoeing
☐ lake   ☐ river   ☐ hot tub
☐ fitness   ☐ bike   ☐ boat
☐ shuffleboard   ☐ pickleball   ☐ golf

Camped with:_____

_____

_____

People met:_____

_____

New friends:_____

_____

Places visited:_____

_____

_____

Visit/do next time:_____

_____

_____

Most memorable event:_____
_____
_____

Most fun things:_____
_____
_____
_____

Notes:_____
_____
_____
_____
_____
_____

Drawing or favorite photo:

Campground: Dates:

Location:_____

Travel to Campground: *Miles:*_____ *Time:*_____ *Cost:*_____

Weather/Temperature:_____

Campground Information

Name:_____

Address:_____

Phone:_____

Site#:_____ Site for next time:_____

Cost:_____ $ ☐ Day ☐ Week ☐ Month

GPS:_____

Rating: ★☆☆☆☆☆☆☆☆☆

Water pressure ★☆☆☆☆   Location ★☆☆☆☆

Cleanliness   ★☆☆☆☆   Site size ★☆☆☆☆

Restrooms   ★☆☆☆☆   Noise   ★☆☆☆☆

Amenities:

☐ easy access   ☐ back-in   ☐ pull-through
☐ water   ☐ pet friendly   ☐ laundry
☐ paved   ☐ sewer   ☐ electricity
☐ 15 amp   ☐ 30 amp   ☐ 50 amp
☐ shade   ☐ pool   ☐ restrooms
☐ store   ☐ picnic table   ☐ fire ring
☐ firewood   ☐ tv   ☐ wifi
☐ security   ☐ ice   ☐ cafe

Activities:

☐ fishing   ☐ hiking   ☐ canoeing
☐ lake   ☐ river   ☐ hot tub
☐ fitness   ☐ bike   ☐ boat
☐ shuffleboard   ☐ pickleball   ☐ golf

Camped with:_____

_____

_____

People met:_____

_____

New friends:_____

_____

Places visited:_____

_____

_____

Visit/do next time:_____

_____

_____

Most memorable event:_____

_____

Most fun things:_____

_____

_____

Notes:_____

_____

_____

_____

_____

Drawing or favorite photo:

Campground: Dates:

Location:_____

Travel to Campground: *Miles:*_____ *Time:*_____ *Cost:*_____

Weather/Temperature:_____

Campground Information

Name:_____

Address:_____

Phone:_____

Site#:_____ Site for next time:_____

Cost:_____ $ ☐ Day ☐ Week ☐ Month

GPS:_____

Rating: ★☆☆☆☆☆☆☆☆☆

Water pressure ★☆☆☆☆ Location ★☆☆☆☆

Cleanliness ★☆☆☆☆ Site size ★☆☆☆☆

Restrooms ★☆☆☆☆ Noise ★☆☆☆☆

Amenities:

☐ easy access ☐ back-in ☐ pull-through
☐ water ☐ pet friendly ☐ laundry
☐ paved ☐ sewer ☐ electricity
☐ 15 amp ☐ 30 amp ☐ 50 amp
☐ shade ☐ pool ☐ restrooms
☐ store ☐ picnic table ☐ fire ring
☐ firewood ☐ tv ☐ wifi
☐ security ☐ ice ☐ cafe

Activities:

☐ fishing ☐ hiking ☐ canoeing
☐ lake ☐ river ☐ hot tub
☐ fitness ☐ bike ☐ boat
☐ shuffleboard ☐ pickleball ☐ golf

Camped with:_____

_____

People met:_____

New friends:_____

Places visited:_____

_____

Visit/do next time:_____

_____

Most memorable event:_____

_____

_____

Most fun things:_____

_____

_____

_____

Notes:_____

_____

_____

_____

_____

Drawing or favorite photo:

Campground:	Dates:

Location:_____

Travel to Campground: *Miles:*_____ *Time:*_____ *Cost:*_____

Weather/Temperature:_____

Campground Information

Name:_____

Address:_____

Phone:_____

Site#:_____ Site for next time:_____

Cost:_____ $ ☐ Day ☐ Week ☐ Month

GPS:_____

Rating: ★☆☆☆☆☆☆☆☆☆

Water pressure ★☆☆☆☆ Location ★☆☆☆☆

Cleanliness ★☆☆☆☆ Site size ★☆☆☆☆

Restrooms ★☆☆☆☆ Noise ★☆☆☆☆

Amenities:

☐ easy access ☐ back-in ☐ pull-through
☐ water ☐ pet friendly ☐ laundry
☐ paved ☐ sewer ☐ electricity
☐ 15 amp ☐ 30 amp ☐ 50 amp
☐ shade ☐ pool ☐ restrooms
☐ store ☐ picnic table ☐ fire ring
☐ firewood ☐ tv ☐ wifi
☐ security ☐ ice ☐ cafe

Activities:

☐ fishing ☐ hiking ☐ canoeing
☐ lake ☐ river ☐ hot tub
☐ fitness ☐ bike ☐ boat
☐ shuffleboard ☐ pickleball ☐ golf

Camped with:_____

_____

People met:_____

_____

New friends:_____

_____

Places visited:_____

_____

Visit/do next time:_____

_____

Most memorable event:_____

_____

Most fun things:_____

_____

_____

Notes:_____

_____

_____

_____

_____

Drawing or favorite photo:

Campground: Dates:

Location:_____

Travel to Campground: *Miles:*_____ *Time:*_____ *Cost:*_____

Weather/Temperature:_____

Campground Information

Name:_____

Address:_____

Phone:_____

Site#:_____ Site for next time:_____

Cost:_____ $ ☐ Day ☐ Week ☐ Month

GPS:_____

Rating: ★☆☆☆☆☆☆☆☆☆

Water pressure ★☆☆☆☆ Location ★☆☆☆☆

Cleanliness ★☆☆☆☆ Site size ★☆☆☆☆

Restrooms ★☆☆☆☆ Noise ★☆☆☆☆

Amenities:

☐ easy access   ☐ back-in   ☐ pull-through
☐ water   ☐ pet friendly ☐ laundry
☐ paved   ☐ sewer   ☐ electricity
☐ 15 amp   ☐ 30 amp   ☐ 50 amp
☐ shade   ☐ pool   ☐ restrooms
☐ store   ☐ picnic table ☐ fire ring
☐ firewood   ☐ tv   ☐ wifi
☐ security   ☐ ice   ☐ cafe

Activities:

☐ fishing   ☐ hiking   ☐ canoeing
☐ lake   ☐ river   ☐ hot tub
☐ fitness   ☐ bike   ☐ boat
☐ shuffleboard ☐ pickleball   ☐ golf

Camped with:_____

_____

_____

People met:_____

_____

New friends:_____

_____

Places visited:_____

_____

_____

Visit/do next time:_____

_____

_____

Most memorable event:_____

_____

_____

Most fun things:_____

_____

_____

Notes:_____

_____

_____

_____

_____

Drawing or favorite photo:

Campground: | Dates:

Location:_____

Travel to Campground: *Miles:*_____ *Time:*_____ *Cost:*_____

Weather/Temperature:_____

Campground Information

Name:_____

Address:_____

Phone:_____

Site#:_____ Site for next time:_____

Cost:_____ $ ☐ Day ☐ Week ☐ Month

GPS:_____

Rating: ★☆☆☆☆☆☆☆☆☆

Water pressure ★☆☆☆☆ Location ★☆☆☆☆

Cleanliness ★☆☆☆☆ Site size ★☆☆☆☆

Restrooms ★☆☆☆☆ Noise ★☆☆☆☆

Amenities:

☐ easy access ☐ back-in ☐ pull-through
☐ water ☐ pet friendly ☐ laundry
☐ paved ☐ sewer ☐ electricity
☐ 15 amp ☐ 30 amp ☐ 50 amp
☐ shade ☐ pool ☐ restrooms
☐ store ☐ picnic table ☐ fire ring
☐ firewood ☐ tv ☐ wifi
☐ security ☐ ice ☐ cafe

Activities:

☐ fishing ☐ hiking ☐ canoeing
☐ lake ☐ river ☐ hot tub
☐ fitness ☐ bike ☐ boat
☐ shuffleboard ☐ pickleball ☐ golf

Camped with:_____

_____

People met:_____

_____

New friends:_____

_____

Places visited:_____

_____

Visit/do next time:_____

_____

Most memorable event:_____

_____

Most fun things:_____

_____

_____

Notes:_____

_____

_____

_____

_____

Drawing or favorite photo:

Campground: Dates:

Location:_____

Travel to Campground: *Miles:*_____ *Time:*_____ *Cost:*_____

Weather/Temperature:_____

Campground Information

Name:_____

Address:_____

Phone:_____

Site#:_____ Site for next time:_____

Cost:_____ $ ☐ Day ☐ Week ☐ Month

GPS:_____

Rating: ★☆☆☆☆☆☆☆☆☆

Water pressure ★☆☆☆☆ Location ★☆☆☆☆

Cleanliness ★☆☆☆☆ Site size ★☆☆☆☆

Restrooms ★☆☆☆☆ Noise ★☆☆☆☆

Amenities:

☐ easy access   ☐ back-in   ☐ pull-through
☐ water   ☐ pet friendly   ☐ laundry
☐ paved   ☐ sewer   ☐ electricity
☐ 15 amp   ☐ 30 amp   ☐ 50 amp
☐ shade   ☐ pool   ☐ restrooms
☐ store   ☐ picnic table   ☐ fire ring
☐ firewood   ☐ tv   ☐ wifi
☐ security   ☐ ice   ☐ cafe

Activities:

☐ fishing   ☐ hiking   ☐ canoeing
☐ lake   ☐ river   ☐ hot tub
☐ fitness   ☐ bike   ☐ boat
☐ shuffleboard ☐ pickleball   ☐ golf

Camped with:_____

_____

People met:_____

New friends:_____

Places visited:_____

_____

Visit/do next time:_____

_____

Most memorable event:_____

_____

_____

Most fun things:_____

_____

_____

_____

Notes:_____

_____

_____

_____

_____

Drawing or favorite photo:

Campground:	Dates:

Location:_____

Travel to Campground: *Miles:*_____ *Time:*_____ *Cost:*_____

Weather/Temperature:_____

Campground Information

Name:_____

Address:_____

Phone:_____

Site#:_____ Site for next time:_____

Cost:_____ $ ☐ Day ☐ Week ☐ Month

GPS:_____

Rating: ★☆☆☆☆☆☆☆☆☆

Water pressure ★☆☆☆☆ Location ★☆☆☆☆

Cleanliness ★☆☆☆☆ Site size ★☆☆☆☆

Restrooms ★☆☆☆☆ Noise ★☆☆☆☆

Amenities:

☐ easy access ☐ back-in ☐ pull-through
☐ water ☐ pet friendly ☐ laundry
☐ paved ☐ sewer ☐ electricity
☐ 15 amp ☐ 30 amp ☐ 50 amp
☐ shade ☐ pool ☐ restrooms
☐ store ☐ picnic table ☐ fire ring
☐ firewood ☐ tv ☐ wifi
☐ security ☐ ice ☐ cafe

Activities:

☐ fishing ☐ hiking ☐ canoeing
☐ lake ☐ river ☐ hot tub
☐ fitness ☐ bike ☐ boat
☐ shuffleboard ☐ pickleball ☐ golf

Camped with:_____

_____

People met:_____

New friends:_____

Places visited:_____

Visit/do next time:_____

Most memorable event: _____

_____

Most fun things: _____

_____

_____

Notes: _____

_____

_____

_____

_____

Drawing or favorite photo:

Campground:	Dates:

Location:_____

Travel to Campground: *Miles:*_____ *Time:*_____ *Cost:*_____

Weather/Temperature:_____

Campground Information

Name:_____

Address:_____

Phone:_____

Site#:_____ Site for next time:_____

Cost:_____ $ ☐ Day ☐ Week ☐ Month

GPS:_____

Rating: ★☆☆☆☆☆☆☆☆☆

Water pressure ★☆☆☆☆ Location ★☆☆☆☆

Cleanliness ★☆☆☆☆ Site size ★☆☆☆☆

Restrooms ★☆☆☆☆ Noise ★☆☆☆☆

Amenities:

☐ easy access ☐ back-in ☐ pull-through
☐ water ☐ pet friendly ☐ laundry
☐ paved ☐ sewer ☐ electricity
☐ 15 amp ☐ 30 amp ☐ 50 amp
☐ shade ☐ pool ☐ restrooms
☐ store ☐ picnic table ☐ fire ring
☐ firewood ☐ tv ☐ wifi
☐ security ☐ ice ☐ cafe

Activities:

☐ fishing ☐ hiking ☐ canoeing
☐ lake ☐ river ☐ hot tub
☐ fitness ☐ bike ☐ boat
☐ shuffleboard ☐ pickleball ☐ golf

Camped with:_____

_____

_____

People met:_____

_____

New friends:_____

_____

Places visited:_____

_____

_____

Visit/do next time:_____

_____

_____

Most memorable event:_____

_____

Most fun things:_____

_____

_____

Notes:_____

_____

_____

_____

_____

Drawing or favorite photo:

Campground:	Dates:

Location:_____

Travel to Campground: *Miles:*_____ *Time:*_____ *Cost:*_____

Weather/Temperature:_____

Campground Information

Name:_____

Address:_____

Phone:_____

Site#:_____ Site for next time:_____

Cost:_____ $ ☐ Day ☐ Week ☐ Month

GPS:_____

Rating: ★☆☆☆☆☆☆☆☆☆

Water pressure ★☆☆☆☆ Location ★☆☆☆☆

Cleanliness ★☆☆☆☆ Site size ★☆☆☆☆

Restrooms ★☆☆☆☆ Noise ★☆☆☆☆

Amenities:

☐ easy access ☐ back-in ☐ pull-through
☐ water ☐ pet friendly ☐ laundry
☐ paved ☐ sewer ☐ electricity
☐ 15 amp ☐ 30 amp ☐ 50 amp
☐ shade ☐ pool ☐ restrooms
☐ store ☐ picnic table ☐ fire ring
☐ firewood ☐ tv ☐ wifi
☐ security ☐ ice ☐ cafe

Activities:

☐ fishing ☐ hiking ☐ canoeing
☐ lake ☐ river ☐ hot tub
☐ fitness ☐ bike ☐ boat
☐ shuffleboard ☐ pickleball ☐ golf

Camped with:_____

_____

_____

People met:_____

_____

New friends:_____

_____

Places visited:_____

_____

_____

Visit/do next time:_____

_____

_____

Most memorable event:_____

_____

_____

Most fun things:_____

_____

_____

_____

Notes:_____

_____

_____

_____

_____

Drawing or favorite photo:

Campground: Dates:

Location:_____

Travel to Campground: *Miles:*_____ *Time:*_____ *Cost:*_____

Weather/Temperature:_____

Campground Information

Name:_____

Address:_____

Phone:_____

Site#:_____ Site for next time:_____

Cost:_____ $ ☐ Day ☐ Week ☐ Month

GPS:_____

Rating: ★☆☆☆☆☆☆☆☆☆

Water pressure ★☆☆☆☆   Location ★☆☆☆☆

Cleanliness ★☆☆☆☆   Site size ★☆☆☆☆

Restrooms ★☆☆☆☆   Noise ★☆☆☆☆

Amenities:

☐ easy access ☐ back-in ☐ pull-through
☐ water ☐ pet friendly ☐ laundry
☐ paved ☐ sewer ☐ electricity
☐ 15 amp ☐ 30 amp ☐ 50 amp
☐ shade ☐ pool ☐ restrooms
☐ store ☐ picnic table ☐ fire ring
☐ firewood ☐ tv ☐ wifi
☐ security ☐ ice ☐ cafe

Activities:

☐ fishing ☐ hiking ☐ canoeing
☐ lake ☐ river ☐ hot tub
☐ fitness ☐ bike ☐ boat
☐ shuffleboard ☐ pickleball ☐ golf

Camped with:_____

People met:_____

New friends:_____

Places visited:_____

Visit/do next time:_____

Most memorable event:_____

_____

_____

Most fun things:_____

_____

_____

_____

Notes:_____

_____

_____

_____

_____

Drawing or favorite photo:

Campground: Dates:

Location:_____

Travel to Campground: *Miles:*_____ *Time:*_____ *Cost:*_____

Weather/Temperature:_____

Campground Information

Name:_____

Address:_____

Phone:_____

Site#:_____ Site for next time:_____

Cost:_____ $ ☐ Day ☐ Week ☐ Month

GPS:_____

Rating: ★☆☆☆☆☆☆☆☆☆

Water pressure ★☆☆☆☆ Location ★☆☆☆☆

Cleanliness ★☆☆☆☆ Site size ★☆☆☆☆

Restrooms ★☆☆☆☆ Noise ★☆☆☆☆

Amenities:

☐ easy access   ☐ back-in   ☐ pull-through
☐ water   ☐ pet friendly   ☐ laundry
☐ paved   ☐ sewer   ☐ electricity
☐ 15 amp   ☐ 30 amp   ☐ 50 amp
☐ shade   ☐ pool   ☐ restrooms
☐ store   ☐ picnic table   ☐ fire ring
☐ firewood   ☐ tv   ☐ wifi
☐ security   ☐ ice   ☐ cafe

Activities:

☐ fishing   ☐ hiking   ☐ canoeing
☐ lake   ☐ river   ☐ hot tub
☐ fitness   ☐ bike   ☐ boat
☐ shuffleboard   ☐ pickleball   ☐ golf

Camped with:_____

_____

_____

People met:_____

New friends:_____

Places visited:_____

_____

_____

Visit/do next time:_____

_____

_____

Most memorable event:_____

_____

_____

Most fun things:_____

_____

_____

_____

Notes:_____

_____

_____

_____

_____

_____

Drawing or favorite photo:

Campground: _____ Dates: _____

Location:_____

Travel to Campground: *Miles:*_____ *Time:*_____ *Cost:*_____

Weather/Temperature:_____

Campground Information

Name:_____

Address:_____

Phone:_____

Site#:_____ Site for next time:_____

Cost:_____ $ ☐ Day ☐ Week ☐ Month

GPS:_____

Rating: ★☆☆☆☆☆☆☆☆☆

Water pressure ★☆☆☆☆ Location ★☆☆☆☆

Cleanliness ★☆☆☆☆ Site size ★☆☆☆☆

Restrooms ★☆☆☆☆ Noise ★☆☆☆☆

Amenities:

☐ easy access ☐ back-in ☐ pull-through
☐ water ☐ pet friendly ☐ laundry
☐ paved ☐ sewer ☐ electricity
☐ 15 amp ☐ 30 amp ☐ 50 amp
☐ shade ☐ pool ☐ restrooms
☐ store ☐ picnic table ☐ fire ring
☐ firewood ☐ tv ☐ wifi
☐ security ☐ ice ☐ cafe

Activities:

☐ fishing ☐ hiking ☐ canoeing
☐ lake ☐ river ☐ hot tub
☐ fitness ☐ bike ☐ boat
☐ shuffleboard ☐ pickleball ☐ golf

Camped with:_____

_____

_____

People met:_____

_____

New friends:_____

_____

Places visited:_____

_____

_____

Visit/do next time:_____

_____

_____

Most memorable event:_____

_____

Most fun things:_____

_____

_____

Notes:_____

_____

_____

_____

_____

Drawing or favorite photo:

Campground: Dates:

Location:_____

Travel to Campground: *Miles:*_____ *Time:*_____ *Cost:*_____

Weather/Temperature:_____

Campground Information

Name:_____

Address:_____

Phone:_____

Site#:_____ Site for next time:_____

Cost:_____ $ ☐ Day ☐ Week ☐ Month

GPS:_____

Rating: ★☆☆☆☆☆☆☆☆☆

Water pressure ★☆☆☆☆ Location ★☆☆☆☆

Cleanliness ★☆☆☆☆ Site size ★☆☆☆☆

Restrooms ★☆☆☆☆ Noise ★☆☆☆☆

Amenities:

☐ easy access   ☐ back-in   ☐ pull-through
☐ water   ☐ pet friendly   ☐ laundry
☐ paved   ☐ sewer   ☐ electricity
☐ 15 amp   ☐ 30 amp   ☐ 50 amp
☐ shade   ☐ pool   ☐ restrooms
☐ store   ☐ picnic table   ☐ fire ring
☐ firewood   ☐ tv   ☐ wifi
☐ security   ☐ ice   ☐ cafe

Activities:

☐ fishing   ☐ hiking   ☐ canoeing
☐ lake   ☐ river   ☐ hot tub
☐ fitness   ☐ bike   ☐ boat
☐ shuffleboard   ☐ pickleball   ☐ golf

Camped with:_____

_____

_____

People met:_____

_____

New friends:_____

_____

Places visited:_____

_____

_____

Visit/do next time:_____

_____

_____

Most memorable event:_____
_____
_____

Most fun things:_____
_____
_____
_____

Notes:_____
_____
_____
_____
_____

Drawing or favorite photo:

Campground:	Dates:

Location:_____

Travel to Campground: *Miles:*_____ *Time:*_____ *Cost:*_____

Weather/Temperature:_____

Campground Information

Name:_____

Address:_____

Phone:_____

Site#:_____ Site for next time:_____

Cost:_____ $ ☐ Day ☐ Week ☐ Month

GPS:_____

Rating: ★☆☆☆☆☆☆☆☆☆

Water pressure ★☆☆☆☆ Location ★☆☆☆☆

Cleanliness ★☆☆☆☆ Site size ★☆☆☆☆

Restrooms ★☆☆☆☆ Noise ★☆☆☆☆

Amenities:

☐ easy access	☐ back-in	☐ pull-through
☐ water	☐ pet friendly	☐ laundry
☐ paved	☐ sewer	☐ electricity
☐ 15 amp	☐ 30 amp	☐ 50 amp
☐ shade	☐ pool	☐ restrooms
☐ store	☐ picnic table	☐ fire ring
☐ firewood	☐ tv	☐ wifi
☐ security	☐ ice	☐ cafe

Activities:

☐ fishing	☐ hiking	☐ canoeing
☐ lake	☐ river	☐ hot tub
☐ fitness	☐ bike	☐ boat
☐ shuffleboard	☐ pickleball	☐ golf

Camped with:_____

_____

People met:_____

_____

New friends:_____

Places visited:_____

_____

Visit/do next time:_____

_____

Most memorable event:_____

_____

Most fun things:_____

_____

_____

Notes:_____

_____

_____

_____

_____

Drawing or favorite photo:

Campground: Dates:

Location:_____

Travel to Campground: *Miles:*_____ *Time:*_____ *Cost:*_____

Weather/Temperature:_____

Campground Information

Name:_____

Address:_____

Phone:_____

Site#:_____ Site for next time:_____

Cost:_____ $ ☐ Day ☐ Week ☐ Month

GPS:_____

Rating: ★☆☆☆☆☆☆☆☆☆

Water pressure ★☆☆☆☆ Location ★☆☆☆☆

Cleanliness ★☆☆☆☆ Site size ★☆☆☆☆

Restrooms ★☆☆☆☆ Noise ★☆☆☆☆

Amenities:

☐ easy access ☐ back-in ☐ pull-through
☐ water ☐ pet friendly ☐ laundry
☐ paved ☐ sewer ☐ electricity
☐ 15 amp ☐ 30 amp ☐ 50 amp
☐ shade ☐ pool ☐ restrooms
☐ store ☐ picnic table ☐ fire ring
☐ firewood ☐ tv ☐ wifi
☐ security ☐ ice ☐ cafe

Activities:

☐ fishing ☐ hiking ☐ canoeing
☐ lake ☐ river ☐ hot tub
☐ fitness ☐ bike ☐ boat
☐ shuffleboard ☐ pickleball ☐ golf

Camped with:_____

_____

_____

People met:_____

_____

New friends:_____

_____

Places visited:_____

_____

_____

Visit/do next time:_____

_____

_____

Most memorable event:_____
_____
_____

Most fun things:_____
_____
_____
_____

Notes:_____
_____
_____
_____
_____

Drawing or favorite photo:

Campground: Dates:

Location:_____

Travel to Campground: *Miles:*_____ *Time:*_____ *Cost:*_____

Weather/Temperature:_____

Campground Information

Name:_____

Address:_____

Phone:_____

Site#:_____ Site for next time:_____

Cost:_____ $ ☐ Day ☐ Week ☐ Month

GPS:_____

Rating: ★☆☆☆☆☆☆☆☆☆

Water pressure ★☆☆☆☆ Location ★☆☆☆☆

Cleanliness ★☆☆☆☆ Site size ★☆☆☆☆

Restrooms ★☆☆☆☆ Noise ★☆☆☆☆

Amenities:

☐ easy access ☐ back-in ☐ pull-through
☐ water ☐ pet friendly ☐ laundry
☐ paved ☐ sewer ☐ electricity
☐ 15 amp ☐ 30 amp ☐ 50 amp
☐ shade ☐ pool ☐ restrooms
☐ store ☐ picnic table ☐ fire ring
☐ firewood ☐ tv ☐ wifi
☐ security ☐ ice ☐ cafe

Activities:

☐ fishing ☐ hiking ☐ canoeing
☐ lake ☐ river ☐ hot tub
☐ fitness ☐ bike ☐ boat
☐ shuffleboard ☐ pickleball ☐ golf

Camped with:_____

_____

_____

People met:_____

_____

New friends:_____

_____

Places visited:_____

_____

_____

Visit/do next time:_____

_____

_____

Most memorable event:_____

_____

_____

Most fun things:_____

_____

_____

Notes:_____

_____

_____

_____

_____

Drawing or favorite photo:

Campground: Dates:

Location:_____

Travel to Campground: *Miles:*_____ *Time:*_____ *Cost:*_____

Weather/Temperature:_____

Campground Information

Name:_____

Address:_____

Phone:_____

Site#:_____ Site for next time:_____

Cost:_____ $ ☐ Day ☐ Week ☐ Month

GPS:_____

Rating: ★☆☆☆☆☆☆☆☆☆

Water pressure ★☆☆☆☆ Location ★☆☆☆☆

Cleanliness ★☆☆☆☆ Site size ★☆☆☆☆

Restrooms ★☆☆☆☆ Noise ★☆☆☆☆

Amenities:

☐ easy access   ☐ back-in   ☐ pull-through
☐ water   ☐ pet friendly   ☐ laundry
☐ paved   ☐ sewer   ☐ electricity
☐ 15 amp   ☐ 30 amp   ☐ 50 amp
☐ shade   ☐ pool   ☐ restrooms
☐ store   ☐ picnic table   ☐ fire ring
☐ firewood   ☐ tv   ☐ wifi
☐ security   ☐ ice   ☐ cafe

Activities:

☐ fishing   ☐ hiking   ☐ canoeing
☐ lake   ☐ river   ☐ hot tub
☐ fitness   ☐ bike   ☐ boat
☐ shuffleboard ☐ pickleball   ☐ golf

Camped with:_____

_____

_____

People met:_____

_____

New friends:_____

_____

Places visited:_____

_____

_____

Visit/do next time:_____

_____

_____

Most memorable event:_____

_____

_____

Most fun things:_____

_____

_____

_____

Notes:_____

_____

_____

_____

_____

_____

Drawing or favorite photo:

Campground: Dates:

Location:_____

Travel to Campground: *Miles:*_____ *Time:*_____ *Cost:*_____

Weather/Temperature:_____

Campground Information

Name:_____

Address:_____

Phone:_____

Site#:_____ Site for next time:_____

Cost:_____ $ ☐ Day ☐ Week ☐ Month

GPS:_____

Rating: ★☆☆☆☆☆☆☆☆☆

Water pressure ★☆☆☆☆ Location ★☆☆☆☆

Cleanliness ★☆☆☆☆ Site size ★☆☆☆☆

Restrooms ★☆☆☆☆ Noise ★☆☆☆☆

Amenities:

☐ easy access ☐ back-in ☐ pull-through
☐ water ☐ pet friendly ☐ laundry
☐ paved ☐ sewer ☐ electricity
☐ 15 amp ☐ 30 amp ☐ 50 amp
☐ shade ☐ pool ☐ restrooms
☐ store ☐ picnic table ☐ fire ring
☐ firewood ☐ tv ☐ wifi
☐ security ☐ ice ☐ cafe

Activities:

☐ fishing ☐ hiking ☐ canoeing
☐ lake ☐ river ☐ hot tub
☐ fitness ☐ bike ☐ boat
☐ shuffleboard ☐ pickleball ☐ golf

Camped with:_____

_____

_____

People met:_____

_____

New friends:_____

_____

Places visited:_____

_____

_____

Visit/do next time:_____

_____

_____

Most memorable event:_____

_____

_____

Most fun things:_____

_____

_____

_____

Notes:_____

_____

_____

_____

_____

Drawing or favorite photo:

Campground:	Dates:

Location:_____

Travel to Campground: *Miles:_____ Time:_____ Cost:_____*

Weather/Temperature:_____

Campground Information

Name:_____

Address:_____

Phone:_____

Site#:_____ Site for next time:_____

Cost:_____ $ ☐ Day ☐ Week ☐ Month

GPS:_____

Rating: ★☆☆☆☆☆☆☆☆☆

Water pressure ★☆☆☆☆ Location ★☆☆☆☆

Cleanliness ★☆☆☆☆ Site size ★☆☆☆☆

Restrooms ★☆☆☆☆ Noise ★☆☆☆☆

Amenities:

☐ easy access ☐ back-in ☐ pull-through
☐ water ☐ pet friendly ☐ laundry
☐ paved ☐ sewer ☐ electricity
☐ 15 amp ☐ 30 amp ☐ 50 amp
☐ shade ☐ pool ☐ restrooms
☐ store ☐ picnic table ☐ fire ring
☐ firewood ☐ tv ☐ wifi
☐ security ☐ ice ☐ cafe

Activities:

☐ fishing ☐ hiking ☐ canoeing
☐ lake ☐ river ☐ hot tub
☐ fitness ☐ bike ☐ boat
☐ shuffleboard ☐ pickleball ☐ golf

Camped with:_____

_____

_____

People met:_____

_____

New friends:_____

_____

Places visited:_____

_____

_____

Visit/do next time:_____

_____

_____

Most memorable event:_____

_____

_____

Most fun things:_____

_____

_____

_____

Notes:_____

_____

_____

_____

_____

Drawing or favorite photo:

Campground: _____ Dates: _____

Location:_____

Travel to Campground: *Miles:*_____ *Time:*_____ *Cost:*_____

Weather/Temperature:_____

Campground Information

Name:_____

Address:_____

Phone:_____

Site#:_____ Site for next time:_____

Cost:_____ $ □ Day □ Week □ Month

GPS:_____

Rating: ★☆☆☆☆☆☆☆☆☆

Water pressure ★☆☆☆☆ Location ★☆☆☆☆

Cleanliness ★☆☆☆☆ Site size ★☆☆☆☆

Restrooms ★☆☆☆☆ Noise ★☆☆☆☆

Amenities:

□ easy access □ back-in □ pull-through
□ water □ pet friendly □ laundry
□ paved □ sewer □ electricity
□ 15 amp □ 30 amp □ 50 amp
□ shade □ pool □ restrooms
□ store □ picnic table □ fire ring
□ firewood □ tv □ wifi
□ security □ ice □ cafe

Activities:

□ fishing □ hiking □ canoeing
□ lake □ river □ hot tub
□ fitness □ bike □ boat
□ shuffleboard □ pickleball □ golf

Camped with:_____

_____

_____

People met:_____

_____

New friends:_____

_____

Places visited:_____

_____

_____

Visit/do next time:_____

_____

_____

Most memorable event:_____

_____

_____

Most fun things:_____

_____

_____

_____

Notes:_____

_____

_____

_____

_____

Drawing or favorite photo:

Campground:	Dates:

Location:_____

Travel to Campground: *Miles:*_____ *Time:*_____ *Cost:*_____

Weather/Temperature:_____

Campground Information

Name:_____

Address:_____

Phone:_____

Site#:_____ Site for next time:_____

Cost:_____ $ ☐ Day ☐ Week ☐ Month

GPS:_____

Rating: ★☆☆☆☆☆☆☆☆☆

Water pressure ★☆☆☆☆ Location ★☆☆☆☆

Cleanliness ★☆☆☆☆ Site size ★☆☆☆☆

Restrooms ★☆☆☆☆ Noise ★☆☆☆☆

Amenities:

☐ easy access ☐ back-in ☐ pull-through
☐ water ☐ pet friendly ☐ laundry
☐ paved ☐ sewer ☐ electricity
☐ 15 amp ☐ 30 amp ☐ 50 amp
☐ shade ☐ pool ☐ restrooms
☐ store ☐ picnic table ☐ fire ring
☐ firewood ☐ tv ☐ wifi
☐ security ☐ ice ☐ cafe

Activities:

☐ fishing ☐ hiking ☐ canoeing
☐ lake ☐ river ☐ hot tub
☐ fitness ☐ bike ☐ boat
☐ shuffleboard ☐ pickleball ☐ golf

Camped with:_____

_____

People met:_____

New friends:_____

Places visited:_____

_____

Visit/do next time:_____

_____

Most memorable event:_____

_____

_____

Most fun things:_____

_____

_____

_____

Notes:_____

_____

_____

_____

_____

_____

Drawing or favorite photo:

Campground: _____ Dates: _____

Location: _____

Travel to Campground: *Miles:* _____ *Time:* _____ *Cost:* _____

Weather/Temperature: _____

Campground Information

Name: _____

Address: _____

Phone: _____

Site#: _____ Site for next time: _____

Cost: _____ $ ☐ Day ☐ Week ☐ Month

GPS: _____

Rating: ★☆☆☆☆☆☆☆☆☆

Water pressure ★☆☆☆☆ Location ★☆☆☆☆

Cleanliness ★☆☆☆☆ Site size ★☆☆☆☆

Restrooms ★☆☆☆☆ Noise ★☆☆☆☆

Amenities:

☐ easy access ☐ back-in ☐ pull-through
☐ water ☐ pet friendly ☐ laundry
☐ paved ☐ sewer ☐ electricity
☐ 15 amp ☐ 30 amp ☐ 50 amp
☐ shade ☐ pool ☐ restrooms
☐ store ☐ picnic table ☐ fire ring
☐ firewood ☐ tv ☐ wifi
☐ security ☐ ice ☐ cafe

Activities:

☐ fishing ☐ hiking ☐ canoeing
☐ lake ☐ river ☐ hot tub
☐ fitness ☐ bike ☐ boat
☐ shuffleboard ☐ pickleball ☐ golf

Camped with: _____

_____

People met: _____

_____

New friends: _____

_____

Places visited: _____

_____

Visit/do next time: _____

_____

Most memorable event:_____

_____

_____

Most fun things:_____

_____

_____

_____

Notes:_____

_____

_____

_____

_____

_____

Drawing or favorite photo:

Campground:	Dates:

Location:_____

Travel to Campground: *Miles:*_____ *Time:*_____ *Cost:*_____

Weather/Temperature:_____

Campground Information

Name:_____

Address:_____

Phone:_____

Site#:_____ Site for next time:_____

Cost:_____ $ ☐ Day ☐ Week ☐ Month

GPS:_____

Rating: ★☆☆☆☆☆☆☆☆☆

Water pressure ★☆☆☆☆ Location ★☆☆☆☆

Cleanliness ★☆☆☆☆ Site size ★☆☆☆☆

Restrooms ★☆☆☆☆ Noise ★☆☆☆☆

Amenities:

☐ easy access ☐ back-in ☐ pull-through
☐ water ☐ pet friendly ☐ laundry
☐ paved ☐ sewer ☐ electricity
☐ 15 amp ☐ 30 amp ☐ 50 amp
☐ shade ☐ pool ☐ restrooms
☐ store ☐ picnic table ☐ fire ring
☐ firewood ☐ tv ☐ wifi
☐ security ☐ ice ☐ cafe

Activities:

☐ fishing ☐ hiking ☐ canoeing
☐ lake ☐ river ☐ hot tub
☐ fitness ☐ bike ☐ boat
☐ shuffleboard ☐ pickleball ☐ golf

Camped with:_____

_____

People met:_____

New friends:_____

Places visited:_____

_____

Visit/do next time:_____

_____

Most memorable event:_____

_____

_____

Most fun things:_____

_____

_____

_____

Notes:_____

_____

_____

_____

_____

Drawing or favorite photo:

Campground: Dates:

Location:_____

Travel to Campground: *Miles:*_____ *Time:*_____ *Cost:*_____

Weather/Temperature:_____

Campground Information

Name:_____

Address:_____

Phone:_____

Site#:_____ Site for next time:_____

Cost:_____ $ ☐ Day ☐ Week ☐ Month

GPS:_____

Rating: ★☆☆☆☆☆☆☆☆☆

Water pressure ★☆☆☆☆ Location ★☆☆☆☆

Cleanliness ★☆☆☆☆ Site size ★☆☆☆☆

Restrooms ★☆☆☆☆ Noise ★☆☆☆☆

Amenities:

☐ easy access ☐ back-in ☐ pull-through
☐ water ☐ pet friendly ☐ laundry
☐ paved ☐ sewer ☐ electricity
☐ 15 amp ☐ 30 amp ☐ 50 amp
☐ shade ☐ pool ☐ restrooms
☐ store ☐ picnic table ☐ fire ring
☐ firewood ☐ tv ☐ wifi
☐ security ☐ ice ☐ cafe

Activities:

☐ fishing ☐ hiking ☐ canoeing
☐ lake ☐ river ☐ hot tub
☐ fitness ☐ bike ☐ boat
☐ shuffleboard ☐ pickleball ☐ golf

Camped with:_____

_____

_____

People met:_____

_____

New friends:_____

_____

Places visited:_____

_____

_____

Visit/do next time:_____

_____

_____

Most memorable event:_____

_____

_____

Most fun things:_____

_____

_____

Notes:_____

_____

_____

_____

_____

Drawing or favorite photo:

Campground: Dates:

Location:_____

Travel to Campground: *Miles:*_____ *Time:*_____ *Cost:*_____

Weather/Temperature:_____

Campground Information

Name:_____

Address:_____

Phone:_____

Site#:_____ Site for next time:_____

Cost:_____ $ ☐ Day ☐ Week ☐ Month

GPS:_____

Rating: ★☆☆☆☆☆☆☆☆☆

Water pressure ★☆☆☆☆ Location ★☆☆☆☆

Cleanliness ★☆☆☆☆ Site size ★☆☆☆☆

Restrooms ★☆☆☆☆ Noise ★☆☆☆☆

Amenities:

☐ easy access ☐ back-in ☐ pull-through
☐ water ☐ pet friendly ☐ laundry
☐ paved ☐ sewer ☐ electricity
☐ 15 amp ☐ 30 amp ☐ 50 amp
☐ shade ☐ pool ☐ restrooms
☐ store ☐ picnic table ☐ fire ring
☐ firewood ☐ tv ☐ wifi
☐ security ☐ ice ☐ cafe

Activities:

☐ fishing ☐ hiking ☐ canoeing
☐ lake ☐ river ☐ hot tub
☐ fitness ☐ bike ☐ boat
☐ shuffleboard ☐ pickleball ☐ golf

Camped with:_____

_____

_____

People met:_____

_____

New friends:_____

_____

Places visited:_____

_____

_____

Visit/do next time:_____

_____

_____

Most memorable event:_____

_____

_____

Most fun things:_____

_____

_____

_____

Notes:_____

_____

_____

_____

_____

Drawing or favorite photo:

Campground: Dates:

Location:_____

Travel to Campground: *Miles:*_____ *Time:*_____ *Cost:*_____

Weather/Temperature:_____

Campground Information

Name:_____

Address:_____

Phone:_____

Site#:_____ Site for next time:_____

Cost:_____ $ ☐ Day ☐ Week ☐ Month

GPS:_____

Rating: ★☆☆☆☆☆☆☆☆☆

Water pressure ★☆☆☆☆ Location ★☆☆☆☆

Cleanliness ★☆☆☆☆ Site size ★☆☆☆☆

Restrooms ★☆☆☆☆ Noise ★☆☆☆☆

Amenities:

☐ easy access ☐ back-in ☐ pull-through
☐ water ☐ pet friendly ☐ laundry
☐ paved ☐ sewer ☐ electricity
☐ 15 amp ☐ 30 amp ☐ 50 amp
☐ shade ☐ pool ☐ restrooms
☐ store ☐ picnic table ☐ fire ring
☐ firewood ☐ tv ☐ wifi
☐ security ☐ ice ☐ cafe

Activities:

☐ fishing ☐ hiking ☐ canoeing
☐ lake ☐ river ☐ hot tub
☐ fitness ☐ bike ☐ boat
☐ shuffleboard ☐ pickleball ☐ golf

Camped with:_____

_____

_____

People met:_____

_____

New friends:_____

_____

Places visited:_____

_____

_____

Visit/do next time:_____

_____

_____

Most memorable event:_____

_____

_____

Most fun things:_____

_____

_____

_____

Notes:_____

_____

_____

_____

_____

Drawing or favorite photo:

Campground: Dates:

Location:_____

Travel to Campground: *Miles:*_____ *Time:*_____ *Cost:*_____

Weather/Temperature:_____

Campground Information

Name:_____

Address:_____

Phone:_____

Site#:_____ Site for next time:_____

Cost:_____ $ ☐ Day ☐ Week ☐ Month

GPS:_____

Rating: ★☆☆☆☆☆☆☆☆☆

Water pressure ★☆☆☆☆ Location ★☆☆☆☆

Cleanliness ★☆☆☆☆ Site size ★☆☆☆☆

Restrooms ★☆☆☆☆ Noise ★☆☆☆☆

Amenities:

☐ easy access   ☐ back-in   ☐ pull-through
☐ water   ☐ pet friendly ☐ laundry
☐ paved   ☐ sewer   ☐ electricity
☐ 15 amp   ☐ 30 amp   ☐ 50 amp
☐ shade   ☐ pool   ☐ restrooms
☐ store   ☐ picnic table ☐ fire ring
☐ firewood   ☐ tv   ☐ wifi
☐ security   ☐ ice   ☐ cafe

Activities:

☐ fishing   ☐ hiking   ☐ canoeing
☐ lake   ☐ river   ☐ hot tub
☐ fitness   ☐ bike   ☐ boat
☐ shuffleboard ☐ pickleball   ☐ golf

Camped with:_____

_____

People met:_____

New friends:_____

Places visited:_____

_____

Visit/do next time:_____

_____

Most memorable event:_____
_____
_____

Most fun things:_____
_____
_____

Notes:_____
_____
_____
_____
_____
_____

Drawing or favorite photo:

Campground: _____ Dates: _____

Location:_____

Travel to Campground: *Miles:*_____ *Time:*_____ *Cost:*_____

Weather/Temperature:_____

Campground Information

Name:_____

Address:_____

Phone:_____

Site#:_____ Site for next time:_____

Cost:_____ $ ☐ Day ☐ Week ☐ Month

GPS:_____

Rating: ★☆☆☆☆☆☆☆☆☆

Water pressure ★☆☆☆☆ Location ★☆☆☆☆

Cleanliness ★☆☆☆☆ Site size ★☆☆☆☆

Restrooms ★☆☆☆☆ Noise ★☆☆☆☆

Amenities:

☐ easy access ☐ back-in ☐ pull-through
☐ water ☐ pet friendly ☐ laundry
☐ paved ☐ sewer ☐ electricity
☐ 15 amp ☐ 30 amp ☐ 50 amp
☐ shade ☐ pool ☐ restrooms
☐ store ☐ picnic table ☐ fire ring
☐ firewood ☐ tv ☐ wifi
☐ security ☐ ice ☐ cafe

Activities:

☐ fishing ☐ hiking ☐ canoeing
☐ lake ☐ river ☐ hot tub
☐ fitness ☐ bike ☐ boat
☐ shuffleboard ☐ pickleball ☐ golf

Camped with:_____

_____

_____

People met:_____

_____

New friends:_____

_____

Places visited:_____

_____

_____

Visit/do next time:_____

_____

_____

Most memorable event:_____

_____

Most fun things:_____

_____

_____

Notes:_____

_____

_____

_____

_____

Drawing or favorite photo:

Campground:

Dates:

Location:_____

Travel to Campground: *Miles:*_____ *Time:*_____ *Cost:*_____

Weather/Temperature:_____

Campground Information

Name:_____

Address:_____

Phone:_____

Site#:_____ Site for next time:_____

Cost:_____ $ ☐ Day ☐ Week ☐ Month

GPS:_____

Rating: ★☆☆☆☆☆☆☆☆☆

Water pressure ★☆☆☆☆ Location ★☆☆☆☆

Cleanliness ★☆☆☆☆ Site size ★☆☆☆☆

Restrooms ★☆☆☆☆ Noise ★☆☆☆☆

Amenities:

☐ easy access ☐ back-in ☐ pull-through
☐ water ☐ pet friendly ☐ laundry
☐ paved ☐ sewer ☐ electricity
☐ 15 amp ☐ 30 amp ☐ 50 amp
☐ shade ☐ pool ☐ restrooms
☐ store ☐ picnic table ☐ fire ring
☐ firewood ☐ tv ☐ wifi
☐ security ☐ ice ☐ cafe

Activities:

☐ fishing ☐ hiking ☐ canoeing
☐ lake ☐ river ☐ hot tub
☐ fitness ☐ bike ☐ boat
☐ shuffleboard ☐ pickleball ☐ golf

Camped with:_____

_____

People met:_____

_____

New friends:_____

_____

Places visited:_____

_____

Visit/do next time:_____

_____

Most memorable event:_____

_____

_____

Most fun things:_____

_____

_____

_____

Notes:_____

_____

_____

_____

_____

Drawing or favorite photo:

Campground: Dates:

Location:_____

Travel to Campground: *Miles:*_____ *Time:*_____ *Cost:*_____

Weather/Temperature:_____

Campground Information

Name:_____

Address:_____

Phone:_____

Site#:_____ Site for next time:_____

Cost:_____ $ ☐ Day ☐ Week ☐ Month

GPS:_____

Rating: ★☆☆☆☆☆☆☆☆☆

Water pressure ★☆☆☆☆ Location ★☆☆☆☆

Cleanliness ★☆☆☆☆ Site size ★☆☆☆☆

Restrooms ★☆☆☆☆ Noise ★☆☆☆☆

Amenities:

☐ easy access   ☐ back-in   ☐ pull-through
☐ water   ☐ pet friendly   ☐ laundry
☐ paved   ☐ sewer   ☐ electricity
☐ 15 amp   ☐ 30 amp   ☐ 50 amp
☐ shade   ☐ pool   ☐ restrooms
☐ store   ☐ picnic table   ☐ fire ring
☐ firewood   ☐ tv   ☐ wifi
☐ security   ☐ ice   ☐ cafe

Activities:

☐ fishing   ☐ hiking   ☐ canoeing
☐ lake   ☐ river   ☐ hot tub
☐ fitness   ☐ bike   ☐ boat
☐ shuffleboard   ☐ pickleball   ☐ golf

Camped with:_____

_____

_____

People met:_____

_____

New friends:_____

_____

Places visited:_____

_____

_____

Visit/do next time:_____

_____

_____

Most memorable event:_____

_____

_____

Most fun things:_____

_____

_____

_____

Notes:_____

_____

_____

_____

_____

_____

Drawing or favorite photo:

Campground: Dates:

Location:_____

Travel to Campground: *Miles:*_____ *Time:*_____ *Cost:*_____

Weather/Temperature:_____

Campground Information

Name:_____

Address:_____

Phone:_____

Site#:_____ Site for next time:_____

Cost:_____ $ ☐ Day ☐ Week ☐ Month

GPS:_____

Rating: ★☆☆☆☆☆☆☆☆☆

Water pressure ★☆☆☆☆ Location ★☆☆☆☆

Cleanliness ★☆☆☆☆ Site size ★☆☆☆☆

Restrooms ★☆☆☆☆ Noise ★☆☆☆☆

Amenities:

☐ easy access   ☐ back-in   ☐ pull-through
☐ water   ☐ pet friendly ☐ laundry
☐ paved   ☐ sewer   ☐ electricity
☐ 15 amp   ☐ 30 amp   ☐ 50 amp
☐ shade   ☐ pool   ☐ restrooms
☐ store   ☐ picnic table ☐ fire ring
☐ firewood   ☐ tv   ☐ wifi
☐ security   ☐ ice   ☐ cafe

Activities:

☐ fishing   ☐ hiking   ☐ canoeing
☐ lake   ☐ river   ☐ hot tub
☐ fitness   ☐ bike   ☐ boat
☐ shuffleboard ☐ pickleball   ☐ golf

Camped with:_____

_____

_____

People met:_____

_____

New friends:_____

_____

Places visited:_____

_____

_____

Visit/do next time:_____

_____

_____

Most memorable event:_____

_____

_____

Most fun things:_____

_____

_____

_____

Notes:_____

_____

_____

_____

_____

_____

Drawing or favorite photo:

Campground:

Dates:

Location:_____

Travel to Campground: *Miles:*_____ *Time:*_____ *Cost:*_____

Weather/Temperature:_____

Campground Information

Name:_____

Address:_____

Phone:_____

Site#:_____ Site for next time:_____

Cost:_____ $ ☐ Day ☐ Week ☐ Month

GPS:_____

Rating: ★☆☆☆☆☆☆☆☆☆

Water pressure ★☆☆☆☆ Location ★☆☆☆☆

Cleanliness ★☆☆☆☆ Site size ★☆☆☆☆

Restrooms ★☆☆☆☆ Noise ★☆☆☆☆

Amenities:

☐ easy access   ☐ back-in   ☐ pull-through
☐ water   ☐ pet friendly   ☐ laundry
☐ paved   ☐ sewer   ☐ electricity
☐ 15 amp   ☐ 30 amp   ☐ 50 amp
☐ shade   ☐ pool   ☐ restrooms
☐ store   ☐ picnic table   ☐ fire ring
☐ firewood   ☐ tv   ☐ wifi
☐ security   ☐ ice   ☐ cafe

Activities:

☐ fishing   ☐ hiking   ☐ canoeing
☐ lake   ☐ river   ☐ hot tub
☐ fitness   ☐ bike   ☐ boat
☐ shuffleboard   ☐ pickleball   ☐ golf

Camped with:_____

_____

People met:_____

_____

New friends:_____

_____

Places visited:_____

_____

_____

Visit/do next time:_____

_____

_____

Most memorable event:_____

_____

Most fun things:_____

_____

_____

Notes:_____

_____

_____

_____

_____

Drawing or favorite photo: